Connected  Mathematics™

Spatial Visualization

Student Edition

Glenda Lappan
James T. Fey
William M. Fitzgerald
Susan N. Friel
Elizabeth Difanis Phillips

PEARSON

Prentice
Hall

Needham, Massachusetts
Upper Saddle River, New Jersey

The Connected Mathematics Project was developed at Michigan State University with the support of National Science Foundation Grant No. MDR 9150217.

This project was supported, in part,
by the
National Science Foundation
Opinions expressed are those of the authors
and not necessarily those of the Foundation

The Michigan State University authors and administration have agreed that all MSU royalties arising from this publication will be devoted to purposes supported by the Department of Mathematics and the MSU Mathematics Education Enrichment Fund.

Photo Acknowledgements: 7 (architect) © Spencer Grant/FPG International; 7 (construction) © Norman R. Rowan/Stock, Boston; 10 © Gene Ahrens/FPG International; 13 © George Holton/Photo Researchers, Inc.; 26 © Arvind Garg/Photo Researchers, Inc.; 35 © Roy Bishop/Stock, Boston; 52 © T. Holton/Superstock, Inc.; 67 © Sam C. Pierson Jr./Photo Researchers, Inc.; 68 © S. Vidler/Superstock, Inc.; 79 © C. Orrico/Superstock, Inc.

ISBN 0-13-180815-X
5 6 7 8 9 10   07 06 05

The Connected Mathematics Project Staff

Project Directors

James T. Fey
University of Maryland

William M. Fitzgerald
Michigan State University

Susan N. Friel
University of North Carolina at Chapel Hill

Glenda Lappan
Michigan State University

Elizabeth Difanis Phillips
Michigan State University

Project Manager

Kathy Burgis
Michigan State University

Technical Coordinator

Judith Martus Miller
Michigan State University

Curriculum Development Consultants

David Ben-Chaim
Weizmann Institute

Alex Friedlander
Weizmann Institute

Eleanor Geiger
University of Maryland

Jane Mitchell
University of North Carolina at Chapel Hill

Anthony D. Rickard
Alma College

Collaborating Teachers/Writers

Mary K. Bouck
Portland, Michigan

Jacqueline Stewart
Okemos, Michigan

Graduate Assistants

Scott J. Baldridge
Michigan State University

Angie S. Eshelman
Michigan State University

M. Faaiz Gierdien
Michigan State University

Jane M. Keiser
Indiana University

Angela S. Krebs
Michigan State University

James M. Larson
Michigan State University

Ronald Preston
Indiana University

Tat Ming Sze
Michigan State University

Sarah Theule-Lubienski
Michigan State University

Jeffrey J. Wanko
Michigan State University

Evaluation Team

Mark Hoover
Michigan State University

Diane V. Lambdin
Indiana University

Sandra K. Wilcox
Michigan State University

Judith S. Zawojewski
National-Louis University

Teacher/Assessment Team

Kathy Booth
Waverly, Michigan

Anita Clark
Marshall, Michigan

Theodore Gardella
Bloomfield Hills, Michigan

Yvonne Grant
Portland, Michigan

Linda R. Lobue
Vista, California

Suzanne McGrath
Chula Vista, California

Nancy McIntyre
Troy, Michigan

Linda Walker
Tallahassee, Florida

Software Developer

Richard Burgis
East Lansing, Michigan

Development Center Directors

Nicholas Branca
San Diego State University

Dianne Briars
Pittsburgh Public Schools

Frances R. Curcio
New York University

Perry Lanier
Michigan State University

J. Michael Shaughnessy
Portland State University

Charles Vonder Embse
Central Michigan University

Special thanks to the students and teachers at these pilot schools!

Baker Demonstration School
Evanston, Illinois

Bertha Vos Elementary School
Traverse City, Michigan

Blair Elementary School
Traverse City, Michigan

Bloomfield Hills Middle School
Bloomfield Hills, Michigan

Brownell Elementary School
Flint, Michigan

Catlin Gabel School
Portland, Oregon

Cherry Knoll Elementary School
Traverse City, Michigan

Cobb Middle School
Tallahassee, Florida

Courtade Elementary School
Traverse City, Michigan

Duke School for Children
Durham, North Carolina

DeVeaux Junior High School
Toledo, Ohio

East Junior High School
Traverse City, Michigan

Eastern Elementary School
Traverse City, Michigan

Eastlake Elementary School
Chula Vista, California

Eastwood Elementary School
Sturgis, Michigan

Elizabeth City Middle School
Elizabeth City, North Carolina

Franklinton Elementary School
Franklinton, North Carolina

Frick International Studies Academy
Pittsburgh, Pennsylvania

Gundry Elementary School
Flint, Michigan

Hawkins Elementary School
Toledo, Ohio

Hilltop Middle School
Chula Vista, California

Holmes Middle School
Flint, Michigan

Interlochen Elementary School
Traverse City, Michigan

Los Altos Elementary School
San Diego, California

Louis Armstrong Middle School
East Elmhurst, New York

McTigue Junior High School
Toledo, Ohio

National City Middle School
National City, California

Norris Elementary School
Traverse City, Michigan

Northeast Middle School
Minneapolis, Minnesota

Oak Park Elementary School
Traverse City, Michigan

Old Mission Elementary School
Traverse City, Michigan

Old Orchard Elementary School
Toledo, Ohio

Portland Middle School
Portland, Michigan

Reizenstein Middle School
Pittsburgh, Pennsylvania

Sabin Elementary School
Traverse City, Michigan

Shepherd Middle School
Shepherd, Michigan

Sturgis Middle School
Sturgis, Michigan

Terrell Lane Middle School
Louisburg, North Carolina

Tierra del Sol Middle School
Lakeside, California

Traverse Heights Elementary School
Traverse City, Michigan

University Preparatory Academy
Seattle, Washington

Washington Middle School
Vista, California

Waverly East Intermediate School
Lansing, Michigan

Waverly Middle School
Lansing, Michigan

West Junior High School
Traverse City, Michigan

Willow Hill Elementary School
Traverse City, Michigan

Contents

Ruins of Montarek

What are some situations in which a three-dimensional model is used to represent a three-dimensional object? What are some situations in which a two-dimensional image or drawing is used to represent a three-dimensional object?

How would you ma a drawing to represe a cube building so th a person looking at yo drawing would know exac what the building looks li

How do you think architects communicate information about three-dimensional buildings with a set of two-dimensional drawings?

We live in a three-dimensional world. You and the objects around you can be measured in three different directions. We call these measures length, width, and height. You can look at any object and ask, "How wide is it?" "How long is it?" and "How tall is it?" Objects from our three-dimensional surroundings are often represented with only two dimensions. For example, when you watch television or look at a photograph, you are seeing two-dimensional images of three-dimensional objects. As an experiment, pick up a book and hold it so that you can only see the front cover. From this view, the book looks two-dimensional; you can see its width and height, but not its depth. Just as 3-D is short for "three-dimensional," 2-D is a short way of saying "two-dimensional."

Sometimes we have to make decisions or gather information about three-dimensional objects from two-dimensional representations. Architects create plans for buildings on paper, which serve as a guide to builders during construction. Some video games require making judgments about moves based on the depth of objects as well as their length and width.

In this unit, you will learn about relationships between two-dimensional building plans and three-dimensional buildings. The plans will help you solve problems and make models of the buildings you encounter. You also learn to make a set of plans to describe a particular building. As you develop your spatial skills, you will solve problems like those on the opposite page.

- Here are the *base outline*, *front view*, and *right view* of a cube building. Can you make a model of the building from cubes?

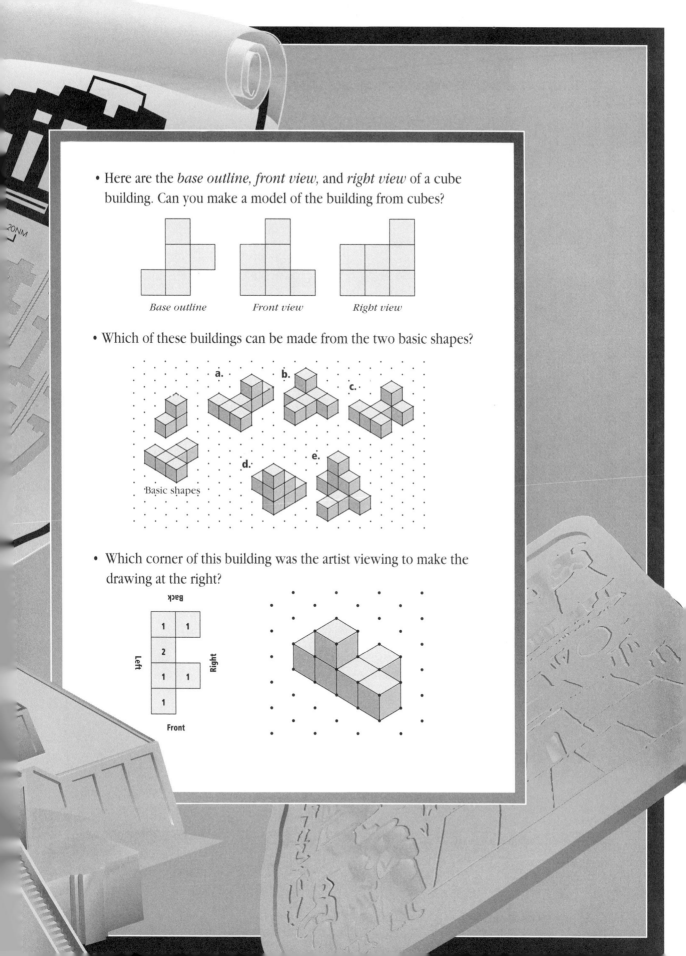

Base outline *Front view* *Right view*

- Which of these buildings can be made from the two basic shapes?

a.

b.

c.

d.

e.

Basic shapes

- Which corner of this building was the artist viewing to make the drawing at the right?

Back

1	1
2	
1	1
1	

Left

Right

Front

Mathematical Highlights

In *Ruins of Montarek,* you will explore relationships between three-dimensional objects and two-dimensional representations of those objects. The unit should help you to

● Create two-dimensional representations of cube buildings in three different ways;

● Understand and recognize line symmetry;

● Read information from two-dimensional drawings and create examples of cube buildings that fit the drawings;

● Understand that a set of drawings or plans can have more than one building that fits the given information and learn to find the maximal and minimal buildings for the plans;

● Visualize transformations of cube buildings and make isometric drawings of the transformed buildings;

● Reason about and communicate spatial relationships; and

● Use models and representations of models of cube buildings to solve problems.

As you work on the problems in this unit, make it a habit to ask questions about situations that involve visualizing and reasoning about three-dimensional objects in space: *What kind of representations might be helpful in understanding the given situation and the relationships among the sets of plans and the buildings in the problem? Will it be useful to look for lines of symmetries in the plans? Are there cubes that are hidden in the buildings that will not be seen in the sets of plans? Do I know where some of the hidden cubes must be in reconstructing the building? Can I visualize what the building looks like from the front and the right side? Can I rotate the building in my head and visualize the other views?*

Building Plans

Have you ever seen a building under construction? As a building crew is constructing a building, they use a set of building plans. *Building plans* show how the different parts of the building—such as the foundation, walls, and ceilings—fit together. Building plans are created by architects and used by building crews and construction supervisors.

In this unit, you will learn about drawings that show what the base and the outside of a building look like. You will also use sets of building plans to construct models of buildings out of cubes. Models tell you how much space is in the building and what it looks like from the outside.

In this unit, Emily Hawkins, a famous explorer and adventurer, investigates the ancient ruins of the lost city of Montarek. As she explores the ruins, Emily finds it helpful to make models of the buildings from cubes. Some of the buildings that once existed in the city are now gone, so making models from the clues that remain is the *only* way to study them.

1.1 Building from Base Plans

The following problems will introduce you to how Emily Hawkins uses sets of plans to describe buildings. You will need 15 cubes and a building mat. A *building mat* is a sheet of paper labeled "Front," "Back," "Left," and "Right" as shown below.

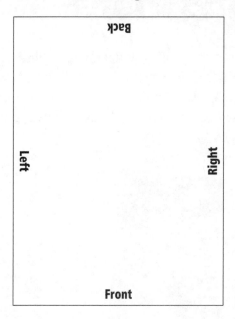

When you make your building mat, put the labels near the edges so there is a large area inside the labels. Always have the building mat on your desk so that the word "Front" is toward you.

One important piece of information to have about a building is the base outline. A *base outline* is a drawing of the building's base. The base outline tells you the shape of the building's base and how many cubes are in the bottom layer. In Problem 1.1, you will be working with a building with this base outline:

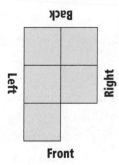

One kind of plan for a building is a simple base plan. A **base plan** is a drawing of the base with numbers on the squares to show how high each stack of cubes is. The building you will be working with in Problem 1.1 has this base plan:

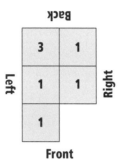

Problem 1.1

The drawings above show the base outline and the base plan for a building. Use the base outline to construct the first layer of the building on your building mat.

How many cubes do you need to construct the bottom layer?

Now use the base plan to complete the building.

If you turn the building mat so that you look at the front, back, left, or right side of your cube building straight on, you will see a two-dimensional pattern of squares. Turn the building on your mat and decide which side of the building (front, back, left, or right) Emily was looking at when she made these diagrams:

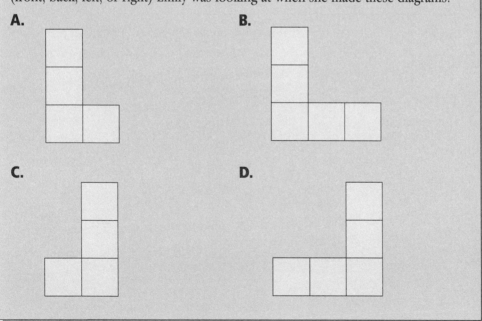

■ Problem 1.1 Follow-Up

1. Compare the four views. What relationships do you see among them? How are they alike and how are they different?

2. If you are on one side of a cube model of a building and your friend is on the opposite side, how do your views of the cube model compare?

3. If your friend shows you a drawing of the back view of a cube model of a building, can you draw the front view? Why or why not?

4. Below is the view of a cube model of a building from the right. What does the left view look like?

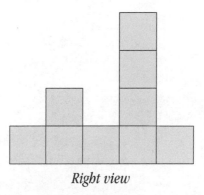

Right view

5. Create a building on your building mat that has the right view shown in question 4. Draw the views from the other three sides of your building. Have your partner check your building and views while you check your partner's.

1.2 Reflecting Figures

A small mirror is useful for visualizing the opposite sides of cube models. You can use a mirror to see the reflection, or *mirror image*, of a given view of a building.

**The Washington Monument and its
reflection in the Tidal Basin**

Labsheet 1.2A shows the figures below. For each drawing, set the edge of a mirror on the mirror line so that the reflecting surface is facing the cube diagram. Sketch the mirror image on the other side of the mirror line, and label the image. If the image is the opposite of the *front*, it must be the *back*. If it is the opposite of the *right*, it must be the *left*.

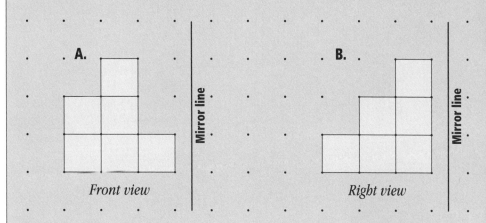

Labsheet 1.2A also shows the polygons below. Try to imagine what the mirror image of each figure would look like. On the labsheet, draw what you think the image will look like. Use a mirror to check your prediction.

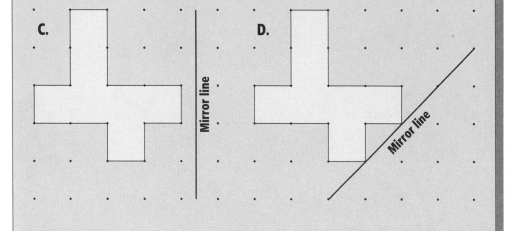

If you made the drawings in Problem 1.2 correctly, they will show *line symmetry* around the mirror line. This means that if you fold your paper on the mirror line, the figure fits exactly on top of its image. Sometimes you can draw a mirror line on the figure itself. If you fold the figure on the mirror line, its two parts fall exactly on top of each other.

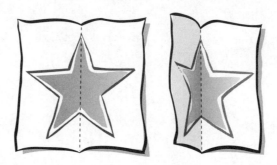

1. On Labsheet 1.2B, see if you can draw mirror lines on the figures shown below.

   a.

   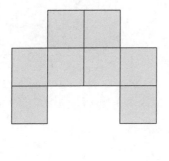

   b.

2. How many different mirror lines can you find for this figure? Use the figure on Labsheet 1.2B and a mirror to test your ideas.

Making Drawings of Cube Models

You can represent a cube building by drawing the base outline and the front, back, left, and right views of the building.

Problem 1.3

Construct this building on your building mat.

A. Draw the base outline of the building on a piece of grid paper. Remember that the base outline shows the cubes that touch the building mat. Then, draw and label the front, back, left, and right views.

Front

B. Remove a cube from the building. Draw a base outline and a set of views for the new building.

C. Return the cube you removed so that you again have the original building. Now, add three more cubes to the building. Draw a base outline and a set of views for the new building.

■ **Problem 1.3 Follow-Up**

Look carefully at your views for each building. For each set of views, do you see any relationships that would let you use fewer views to represent the same information about the building?

Did you know?

The area that is now Central America and southern Mexico was once the home of an ancient people called the Maya. The Mayan civilization flourished between A.D. 250 and A.D. 900. The Maya made extraordinary advancements in astronomy, mathematics, and architecture. Mayan architects created remarkable buildings, including tall limestone pyramids topped by temples, like the one shown at right. Priests climbed the stairs of these pyramids and performed ceremonies in the temples.

1.4 Unraveling Mysteries

Emily Hawkins is trying to unravel some old mysteries about the ruins of the ancient city of Montarek (pronounced *mon tar´ek*). At the site of the ruins, she discovered pieces of broken stone tablets that have parts of sketches and diagrams etched on them. Emily needs to decipher the etchings to reconstruct the entire set of diagrams and sketches.

Problem 1.4

Some of the stone fragments show the front and right views of a building from the ancient city of Montarek.

A. The etchings show this front view of the building:

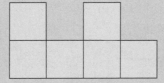

On your grid paper, draw the back view.

B. The etchings show this right view of the building:

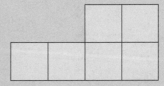

On your grid paper, draw the left view.

C. Use your cubes to build a building that matches your four views.

D. Do you think there is more than one building with the front and right views etched on the tablets and the back and left views you have sketched on grid paper? Explain your answer.

■ Problem 1.4 Follow-Up

Describe in *words* how what you see looking at a cube building from the front compares to what you see looking at the cube building from the back.

1.5 Matching a Building to Its Plans

In the last problem, you found that the right view of a cube building is the mirror image of the left view. Once you see the right view of a cube building, the left view does not give you any new information. Therefore, the plans for a cube building need only contain one of these views. For the same reason, a set of plans need only contain the front view or the back view, not both.

When Emily refers to a **set of building plans,** she is talking about a set of three diagrams—the front view, the right view, and the base outline.

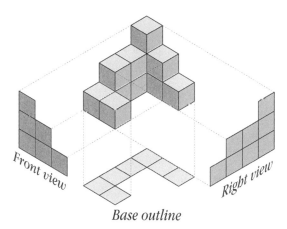

Base outline

Problem 1.5

Emily found a fragment of a stone tablet with this base plan etched on it:

Front

On your building mat, construct the building represented by the base plan.

Emily also found the three sets of building plans shown on the next page on stone tablets. Does one of the three sets of plans correspond to the building you made using the base plan? If so, which one?

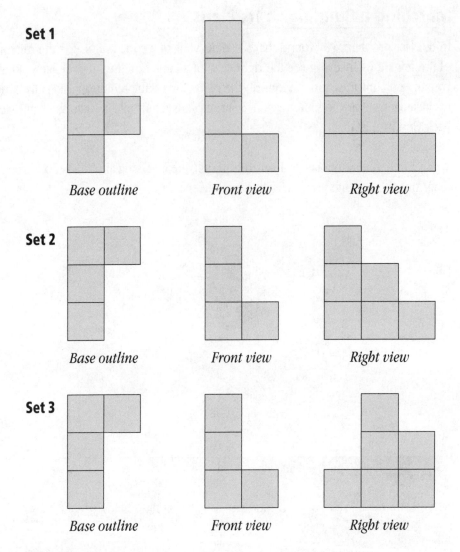

Set 1

Base outline   *Front view*   *Right view*

Set 2

Base outline   *Front view*   *Right view*

Set 3

Base outline   *Front view*   *Right view*

■ **Problem 1.5 Follow-Up**

Examine the sets of plans that do not match the building. Explain why each of these sets of plans does not match.

1.6 **Which Building Is Which?**

In this problem, you will have a chance to test your observation skills. You will try to match four different buildings with their building plans. In order to "read" information about buildings from drawings, you need to be very observant and look carefully at both the drawings and the building.

Below are base plans for four different buildings. With your group, construct a model of each building on a building mat.

A.

2	1	2
2	3	
2	1	

Front

B.

1	1	2
3	1	
2	1	

Front

C.

2	1	1
3	2	
1	1	

Front

D.

1	2	1
2	3	
1	1	

Front

Now, use your observation skills to match your buildings with the drawings on the next page. When you are finished, discuss your ideas with your group and try to reach consensus about which views go with which building.

■ **Problem 1.6 Follow-Up**

1. Can you remove cubes from the building in part A without changing its building plans? Explain your answer.

2. Can you remove cubes from the building in part B without changing its building plans? Explain your answer.

3. Can you remove cubes from the building in part C without changing its building plans? Explain your answer.

4. Can you remove cubes from the building in part D without changing its building plans? Explain your answer.

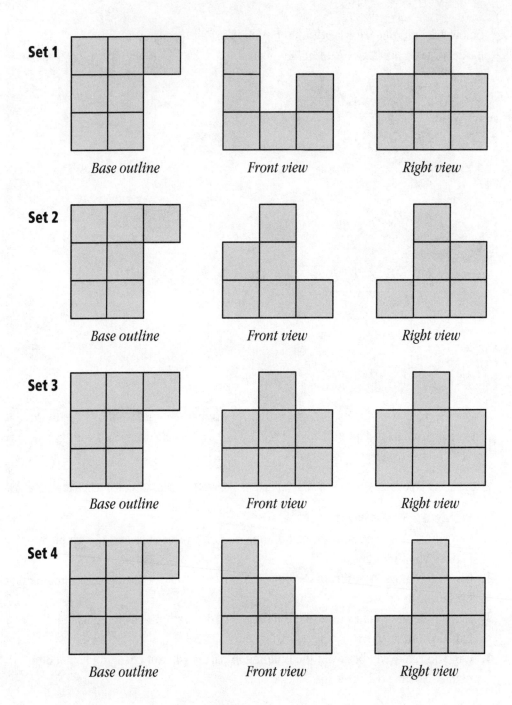

Set 1

Base outline   Front view   Right view

Set 2

Base outline   Front view   Right view

Set 3

Base outline   Front view   Right view

Set 4

Base outline   Front view   Right view

As you work on these ACE questions, use your calculator whenever you need it.

Applications

In 1–4, make a cube model of the building represented by the base plan. Then, make a set of building plans for the building on grid paper. Remember that a *set of building plans* includes a base outline and the front and right views of the building.

1.

1	1	1
1	1	
2		

Front

2.

2	2	1
	3	1
		1

Front

3.

2	1	1
	3	1
	2	

Front

4.

2	3	1
	1	2
	1	

Front

In 5–7, make a cube model of the building represented by the base plan. Then, match the building with the correct set of plans.

5.

1	1	1	1
2	3	3	
	2		

Front

6.

1	3	2	3
1	2	1	
	1		

Front

7.

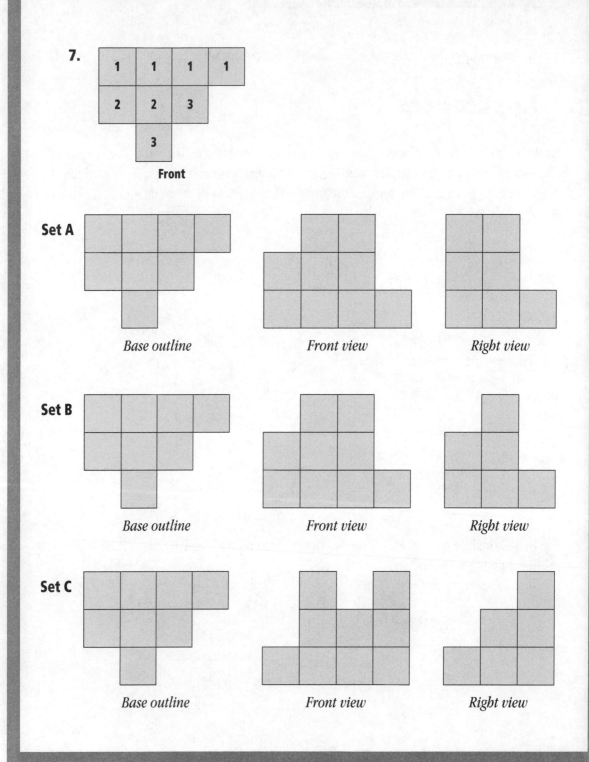

1	1	1	1

2	2	3

3

Front

Set A

Base outline   *Front view*   *Right view*

Set B

Base outline   *Front view*   *Right view*

Set C

Base outline   *Front view*   *Right view*

8. Each side of a number cube is numbered 1, 2, 3, 4, 5, or 6. The numbers are placed so that opposite sides add to 7. Below is the outline of a number cube with some values marked. What should the values of a, b, and c be so that the outline will fold up into a number cube?

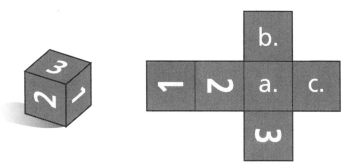

Connections

In 9 and 10, look back at the building plans you made in ACE questions 1 and 3.

9. If the length of a side of each square shown on your building plans is 1 unit, what is the perimeter of each of the three diagrams—base outline, front view, and right view—in each set of building plans for ACE questions 1 and 3?

10. If you were to paint the *top* of each exposed cube on the cube model in ACE question 1, how many square units would you have to paint?

Extensions

11. Emily Hawkins says that in the ancient city of Montarek, different kinds of buildings served different purposes. For example, some buildings were constructed to be garden houses, and others were built to be watchtowers.

   a. Garden houses needed lots of floor space so plants could be displayed and people would have room to walk through the gardens. Draw a base plan for a building that uses eight cubes that you think best meets this requirement for lots of floor space.

   b. Watchtowers needed to be tall but did not need much floor space. Draw a base plan for a building that uses eight cubes that you think would best suit the requirements for a watchtower.

In 12–14, three views of a cube and a sketch of a flattened cube are shown. Copy the sketch of the flattened cube on a sheet of grid paper. Then, use information from the pictures to mark the squares so that, if you folded the sketch into a cube, it would match the drawings.

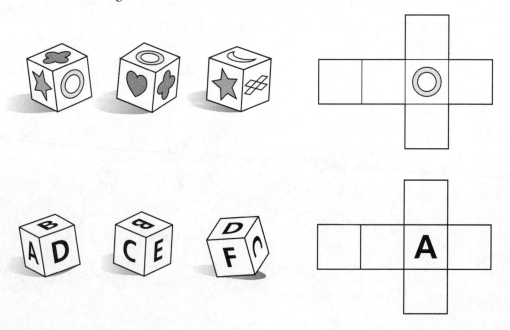

14.

   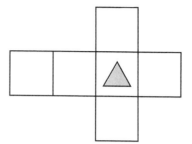

15. Design a cube puzzle of your own.

   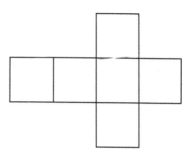

In 16 and 17, use Labsheet 1.ACE. Complete each diagram so that it has line symmetry around the mirror line shown.

16.

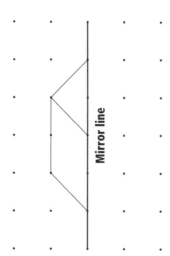

17.

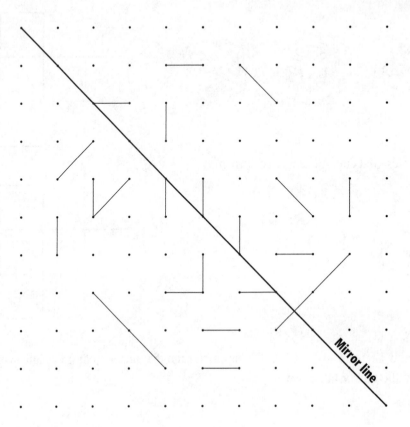

Mirror line

18. Design a figure on dot paper that has at least one line of symmetry.

Mathematical Reflections

In this investigation, you have been learning to read information about three-dimensional buildings from two-dimensional drawings. These questions will help you summarize what you have learned:

1 How does what you see looking at the front of a cube model compare to what you see looking at the back of the cube model?

2 What does it mean for a figure to have *line symmetry?* Give an example as a part of your explanation.

3 How many lines of symmetry does a 3-sided regular polygon have? A 4-sided regular polygon? A 5-sided regular polygon? A 12-sided regular polygon? How do you know your answers are correct?

4 Why is it possible to describe a building with a set of only three drawings—the base outline, the front view, and the right view—rather than a set of views showing each of the four sides and a base outline?

Think about your answers to these questions, discuss your ideas with other students and your teacher, and then write a summary of your findings in your journal.

Making Buildings

In the last investigation, you learned how to draw plans for cube buildings. In this investigation, you will begin by solving mysteries about some ancient buildings. Then, you will construct buildings based on complete and incomplete sets of building plans. By comparing your buildings with those of your classmates, you will determine whether more than one building can be constructed from a set of plans.

2.1 Reconstructing Ruins

For an explorer like Emily Hawkins, carefully analyzing plans of ancient buildings is one way of learning about the culture of the people who once inhabited a city. In this problem, Emily is trying to answer some questions about two buildings that were discovered among the ruins of Montarek.

Did you know?

People lived in "modern" cities over 4000 years ago. In 1922, archaeologists discovered the ruins of the ancient city of Mohenjo-Daro in Pakistan. This city was laid out on a grid containing broad central boulevards with shops. In the city was a huge building where wheat and barley were stored. Some archaeologists believe this building was similar to a modern bank. Many of the estimated 40,000 residents of Mohenjo-Daro lived in private houses with indoor plumbing. This luxury was made possible by an extensive sewer system, which was maintained by public workers.

In A and B, construct the building represented by the base plan. Then, make a set of building plans for each building on grid paper. Remember that a set of building plans consists of the base outline, the front view, and the right view.

A.

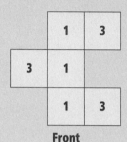

Front

B.

Front

C. Emily has studied some ancient writings she found among the ruins of Montarek. She thinks that one of the two buildings was used as a lookout post to watch for the approach of enemies or friendly travelers. Look at your building plans of the two buildings. Which do you think might have been used as a lookout post? Write at least two or three sentences to explain your answer.

D. Emily has discovered part of a diary kept by one of the residents of ancient Montarek. The diary indicates that the resident lived in the building from part A. Emily shows you a translated entry from the diary:

> *After dinner I went upstairs to my room. The stars were very bright, so I made my way to the tower from where I gazed at the stars. I can look down on the roof of my room from the tower, but I cannot see the tower from the windows of my room.*

By examining your cube model from part A, the building plans you made for the building, and clues from the diary entry, identify which cube(s) on the building might have been the location of the resident's room. Write an explanation for your answer.

■ **Problem 2.1 Follow-Up**

Design a building and imagine that your room is in one of the cubes. Write a diary entry that could be used to figure out where your room is located.

2.2 Constructing Buildings from Plans

So far, you have been drawing sets of building plans by looking at cube models of buildings. Sometimes it is necessary to work the other way. In the next problem, you get to be the explorer and make cube models of buildings from sets of building plans.

Problem 2.2

Emily Hawkins uncovered six ancient stone tablets in her last expedition to the ruins of Montarek. A set of building plans is drawn on each tablet. The plans are shown below and on the next page. Use cubes to make a model of a building corresponding to each set of plans.

As you make each building, compare your models with those of other students in your class. Note how the other cube models are like yours and how they are different. Record a base plan for each building so that you can share what you did with the class.

Set A

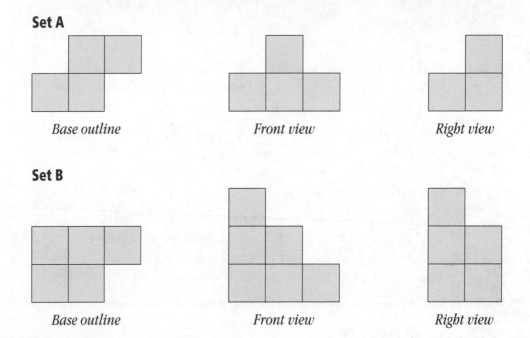

Base outline   Front view   Right view

Set B

Base outline   Front view   Right view

Set C

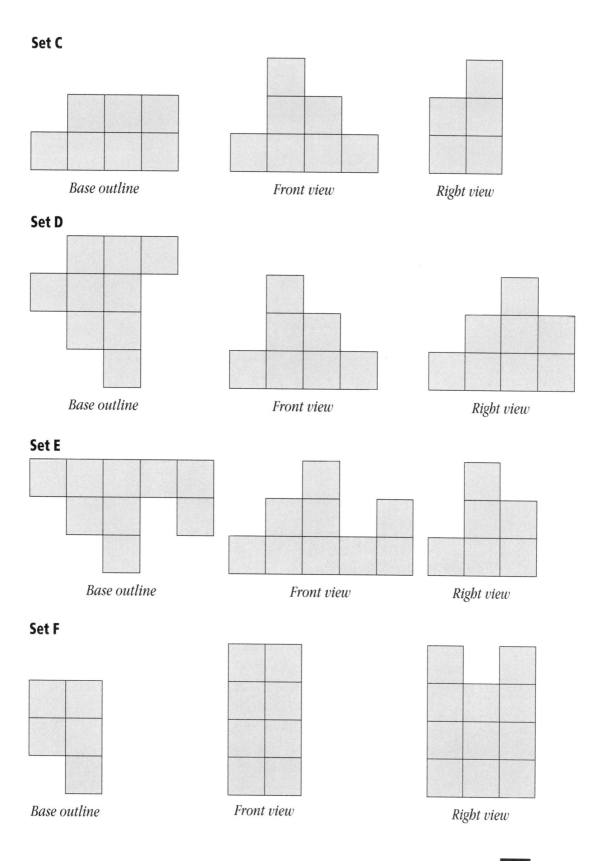

Base outline

Front view

Right view

Set D

Base outline

Front view

Right view

Set E

Base outline

Front view

Right view

Set F

Base outline

Front view

Right view

■ Problem 2.2 Follow-Up

1. Did you find any differences between the cube buildings you made from the building plans and the buildings others in your class made? If so, describe the differences.

2. Do you think that more than one building can be made from a set of building plans? Explain your answer.

2.3 Building from Incomplete Plans

Often Emily finds only partial sets of building plans. She uses these incomplete plans to construct *possible* buildings. In the next problem, you will be working from some of Emily's incomplete sets of building plans.

Did you know?

Architects often prepare blueprints of building plans. A *blueprint* is like a combination of a drawing and a photograph. An architect or builder draws his plans in pencil or India ink on special paper that lets light pass through. This drawing is placed on blueprint paper and exposed to strong light. Special chemicals on the blueprint paper react with the light and turn blue. Because the light does not pass through the lines drawn in pencil or ink, they stay white on the blueprint paper. Before the blueprint is used, it is washed in water to remove the chemicals. This ensures that the white lines do not turn blue when the blueprint is used in the light. Blueprints allow architects and builders to make hundreds of exact copies of building plans for clients and workers.

Emily discovered some pieces of pottery among the ruins of Montarek. Each piece of pottery has an incomplete set of building plans painted on it.

An incomplete set of plans is shown in A–C. In each case, one of the three diagrams is missing—either the base outline, the front view, or the right view. On grid paper, draw the missing view and a base plan for each building.

A.

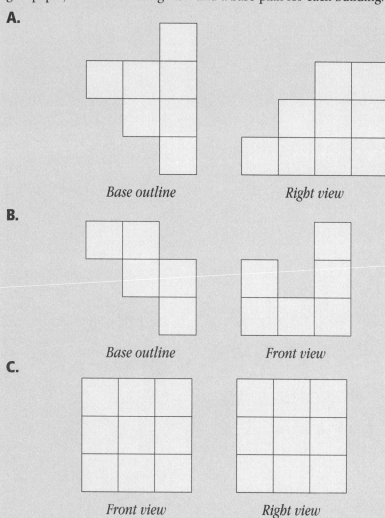

Base outline · Right view

B.

Base outline · Front view

C.

Front view · Right view

D. What is the greatest number of cubes you can use and still fit the plans given in part C? Make a base plan for a building with the greatest number of cubes.

E. What is the least number of cubes you can use and still fit the plans given in part C? Make a base plan for a building with the least number of cubes.

Problem 2.3 Follow-Up

1. Which incomplete set of building plans was easiest to use to create a base plan? Why do you think this is so?
2. Which incomplete set of building plans was hardest to use to create a base plan? Why do you think this is so?
3. Do you think there is more than one base plan possible for a set of incomplete building plans? Why or why not?
4. Compare the base plans you made in part C of the problem with the base plans made by other students in your class. Are your base plans the same or different? Explain your thinking.

As you work on these ACE questions, use your calculator whenever you need it.

Applications

1. Using your cubes, construct the building shown by this base plan:

3	2	2
2	1	2
2	2	3

Front

    a. Draw a set of building plans for the building on grid paper. Remember that a set of building plans includes the base outline, the front view, and the right view.

    b. Modify your cube building to make a different building with the same building plans. Make the base plan for your new building.

    c. Explain how your new building can have the same building plans as the original building even though it has a different base plan.

2. Record a base plan for this building:

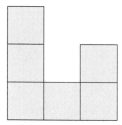
Base outline

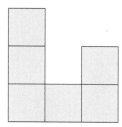
Front view

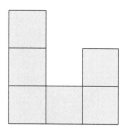
Right view

In questions 3–5, an incomplete set of building plans is given. On grid paper, draw the missing part of the plans—front view, right view, or base outline—and record a base plan for your building.

3.

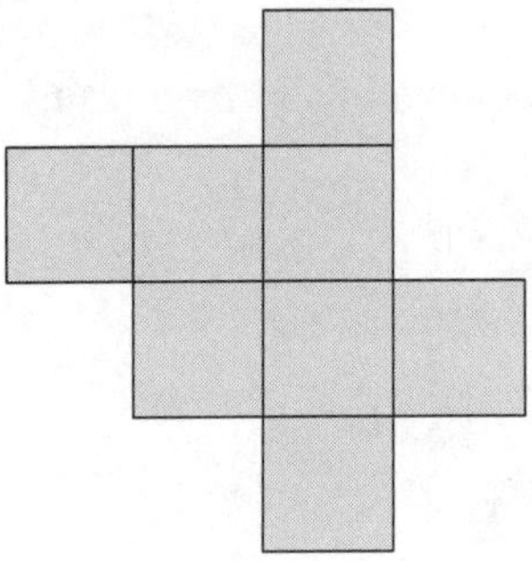

Base outline 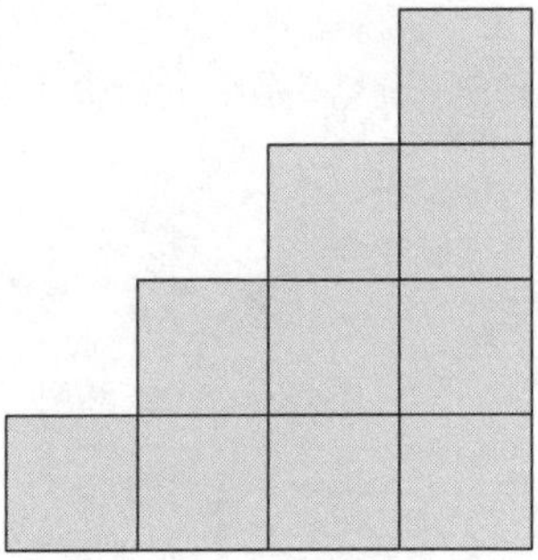   *Right view*

4.

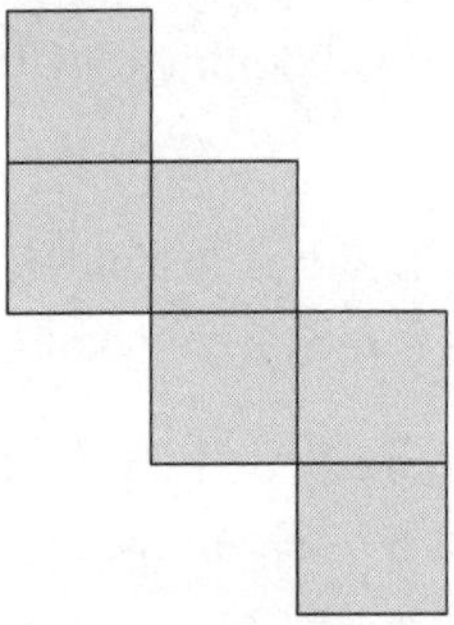

Base outline 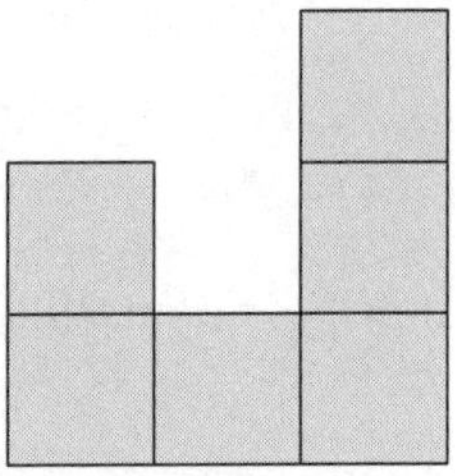   *Front view*

5.

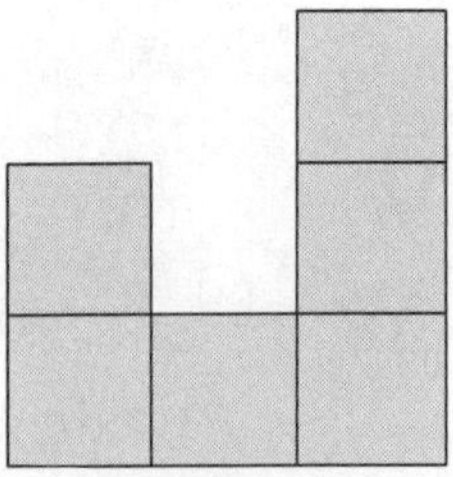

Front view 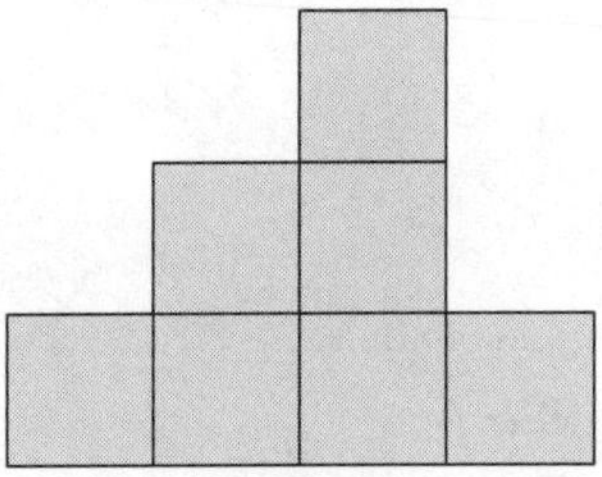   *Right view*

**Ruins of the Propylaea and the Temple of
Athena Nike (427–424 B.C.) in Athens, Greece**

6. Use your cubes to construct the building shown in this base plan:

3	1	1
1	1	2
1		

Front

a. Draw a set of building plans for the building on grid paper.

b. Remove two cubes from the building so that the front view is unchanged.
Make a base plan of the new building.

c. Rebuild the original building. Remove one cube so that the right view *and* the
front view are unchanged. Make a base plan of the new building.

d. Rebuild the original building. What is the greatest number of cubes you can
remove so that the base outline is unchanged? Explain your answer, and make
a base plan of the new building.

Connections

7. The *average height* of a cube building is the mean of the numbers of cubes that are stacked on each square of the building's base outline. Look at this base plan:

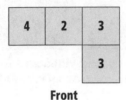

Front

a. Find the average height of this building. Explain how you found your answer.

b. Is it necessary to construct the building with cubes to find the average height? Why or why not?

c. If you multiply the average height of the building by the number of squares in the base outline, what is the result? Is anything special about this number?

d. Find the average height of the building shown in ACE question 2. What does your answer mean?

In 8–10, make a drawing that shows all lines of symmetry for the figure.

8.

9.

10.

Extensions

11. Emily Hawkins has uncovered a stone tablet that describes an ancient building. Emily asks you to help her figure out what the building may have looked like. She shows you this passage, which has been translated from the writing on the tablet:

A building stands at the border of Montarek. The building is made from 12 cubic blocks of stone. Its foundation occupies a rectangular area of 6 square units. Two towers, each made from 4 cubic blocks of stone, reach into the air from opposite corners of the building.

a. Use cubes to make a model of what the building might have looked like. Assume that each face of a cube is 1 square unit of area. Make a base plan of your building, and describe how you figured out how to make your building.

b. Are you sure your building is exactly what the ancient building looked like, or are there other possibilities? Explain your answer.

12. Design a building with no more than 15 cubes. Try to make your building a challenge. Draw a set of plans for your building, including a base outline, a front view, and a right view. Also make a base plan for your building. If there is more than one building that fits your plans, draw a base plan for at least one of these buildings.

Mathematical Reflections

In this investigation, you have learned to use building plans—the base outline, the front view, and the right view—to construct a cube model of a building. Sometimes you made a building from a complete set of plans; other times, one of the views was missing. When you constructed a building from a set of building plans, your building was sometimes different from the buildings made by other students. These questions will help you summarize what you have learned:

1. When you are building from an incomplete set of plans, which piece of information is the hardest to do without: the base outline, the front view, or the right view? Why?

2. If you are given the front view and the right view but not the base outline, how can you always figure out what is the largest possible base that will fit the two views? Explain. Use an example if it helps to explain your thinking.

3. Fatima thinks she has found a good way to build a cube building from a complete set of plans. She builds the base, the right side, and the front side separately and then tries to put them together. What do you think of her method? Will it always work? Why or why not?

Think about your answers to these questions, discuss your ideas with other students and your teacher, and then write a summary of your findings in your journal.

Describing Unique Buildings

In the last investigation, you found that it is sometimes possible to construct more than one building from a set of building plans. We need a way to interpret building plans so that they specify only one building. That way, if you and a friend work independently but use the same set of building plans as a guide, you will construct identical buildings.

3.1 Finding All the Possibilities

In this problem, you will work with your group to find all the buildings that fit a set of building plans.

Problem 3.1

With your cubes, make a building that corresponds to this set of building plans:

Base outline   *Front view*   *Right view*

A. Draw the base plan of your building. Compare your base plan with the base plans made by other students in your group.

B. How many different buildings can be made from this set of building plans? Work with your group until you are sure you have found all of the different buildings. Draw a base plan for each building.

■ Problem 3.1 Follow-Up

1. Of the different base plans you made in Problem 3.1, are there any squares with numbers that do not change? If so, identify the squares with numbers that always remain the same.

2. Look carefully at the base plans for the different buildings you found in Problem 3.1.
   a. What is the least number of cubes used for any of the buildings?
   b. How many different buildings can be made from the least number of cubes?
   c. What is the greatest number of cubes used for any of the buildings?
   d. How many buildings can be made from the greatest number of cubes?

3.2 Finding Maximal and Minimal Buildings

Emily Hawkins has translated some interesting facts about the way buildings were constructed in ancient Montarek. For a set of building plans, buildings made using the *least* number of cubes are called **minimal buildings**. Buildings made with the *greatest* number of cubes are called **maximal buildings**.

In Problem 3.1, you discovered that the *maximal building is unique* and *the minimal building is not necessarily unique*. This means that only one maximal building can be made from a set of building plans. However, using the same plans, it may be possible to construct more than one minimal building.

Problem 3.2

The plans in A–C were discovered by Emily among the ruins of Montarek. For each set of plans, find a minimal building and the maximal building. Record the base plans for your minimal building and the maximal building on grid paper. For each part, compare your minimal and maximal base plans with those of others in your class or group.

A.

Base outline   Front view   Right view

B.

Base outline   Front view   Right view

C.

Base outline   Front view   Right view

■ Problem 3.2 Follow-Up

Create a set of building plans for which the minimal building is the same as the maximal building.

Unraveling an Ancient Mystery

Emily Hawkins' explorations of the ruins of Montarek have helped her to make an important discovery! She discovered that when making a building from a set of building plans, the people of Montarek always constructed the maximal building. Emily feels that this discovery can be useful in solving another ancient mystery about the ruins of Montarek.

In her explorations, Emily came across the following set of building plans for a large and mysterious ancient building:

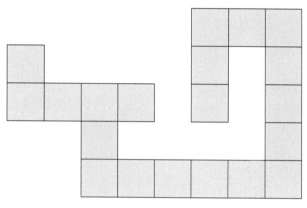

Base outline

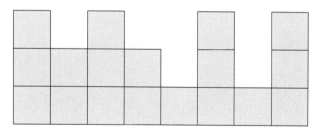

Front view

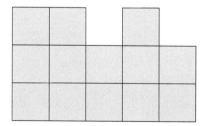

Right view

Problem 3.3

A. Work with your group to construct a minimal building from the set of building plans. Make a base plan of your building on grid paper.

B. Work with your group to construct the maximal building from the set of building plans. Make a base plan of your building on grid paper.

■ Problem 3.3 Follow-Up

Recall that the people of Montarek always constructed maximal buildings. How might the people of Montarek have used this ancient building? Explain your reasoning.

As you work on these ACE questions, use your calculator whenever you need it.

Applications

1. Look carefully at this set of building plans:

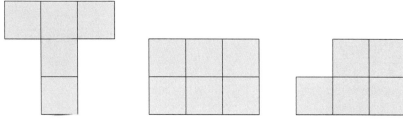

Base outline   *Front view*   *Right view*

a. Construct a minimal building from the building plans. Make a base plan of the building.

b. Suppose it costs $5 to put a special glaze on the top of each exposed cube in a building. How much would it cost to put the glaze on the exposed top of your minimal building?

c. Now construct the maximal building from the building plans. Make a base plan of the building.

d. How much will it cost to glaze the exposed top of the maximal building?

e. How do the costs of glazing the roofs of the minimal and maximal buildings compare? Will the relationship between the cost of glazing the roof of a minimal building and the cost of glazing the roof of a maximal building always be the same as what you found here? Why or why not?

In 2 and 3, make base plans for a minimal building and the maximal building with the given set of building plans. Tell how many cubes are needed for each building.

2.

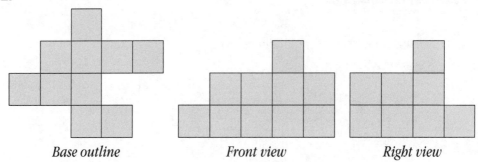

Base outline   *Front view*   *Right view*

3.

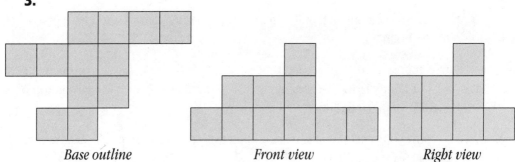

Base outline   *Front view*   *Right view*

Connections

4. Use your cubes to construct a maximal building that has a roof area of 12 square units.

    a. On grid paper, make a base plan of your maximal building, and draw a set of building plans for it.

    b. How many cubes did you use to construct your building?

5. Construct a building with 10 cubes.

    a. On grid paper, make a base plan for your building, and draw a set of building plans for it.

    b. Do you think your building is a minimal building, the maximal building, or neither? Explain your reasoning.

6. Here is a set of incomplete plans for a building.

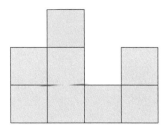 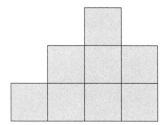

              Base outline   *Front view*

    a. Build every possible building that will fit these plans. Make base plans to record each possible building.

    b. Explain how you know you have found every possible building.

Extensions

7. Emily Hawkins has uncovered another mystery among the ruins of Montarek. She is trying to reconstruct an ancient building that has completely disappeared— no trace of it remains. One of the clues that Emily has is that the building was a maximal building made from 13 cubes. Emily also has a piece of ancient parchment that shows the front view of the building:

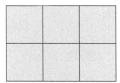

Front view

a. Using your cubes, construct a building that fits the clues. Draw a base plan of the building on grid paper.

b. Make a set of building plans for your building.

c. Do you think the building you have constructed is a model of the same building that once existed in Montarek, or do you think there are other possibilities? Explain your reasoning.

8. a. For each of the regular polygons shown below, find the number of lines of symmetry. Organize your data into a table.

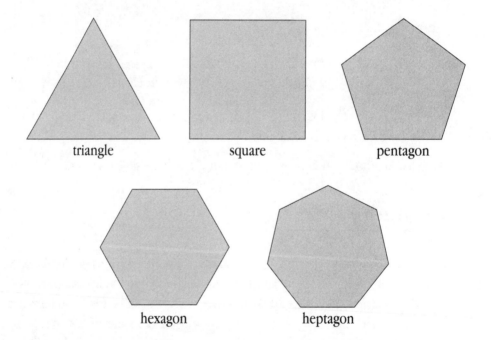

triangle   square   pentagon

hexagon   heptagon

b. Find a pattern in your data that will help you predict how many lines of symmetry a regular polygon with 20 sides will have. Describe your method of predicting.

c. How many lines of symmetry will a regular polygon with 101 sides have?

In 9 and 10, a set of plans for a building is given. The buildings are unusual in that some of the cubes on certain levels fit on half of a cube in the level below. This means that if you look at the building from the top, what you see is not a picture of the base outline. For each building, try to construct the maximal building that fits the plans. Find a way to record your building on paper.

9.

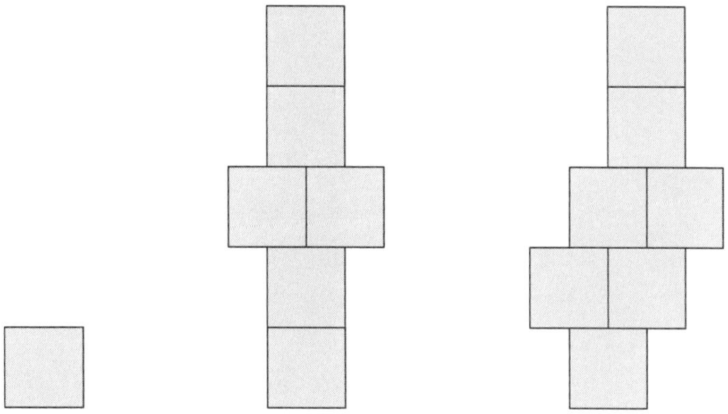

Base outline   Front view   Right view

10.

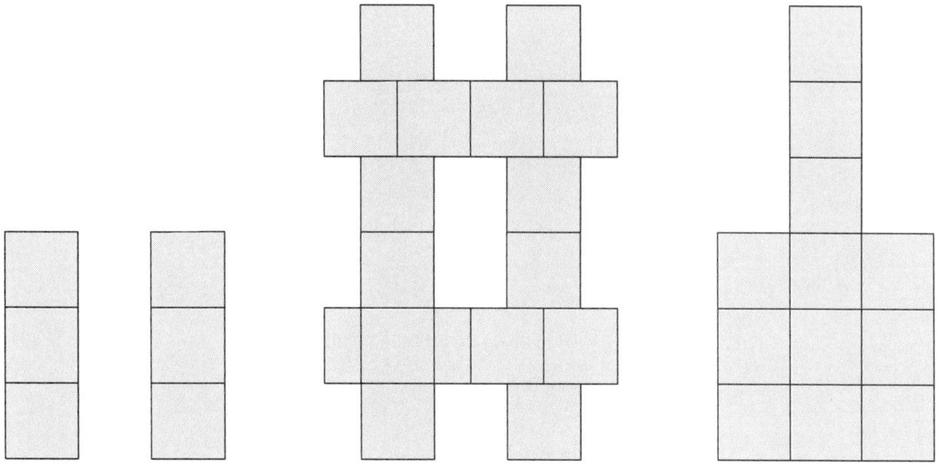

Base outline   Front view   Right view

11. Use exactly 20 cubes to make a model from the building plans below. Record a base plan for your building.

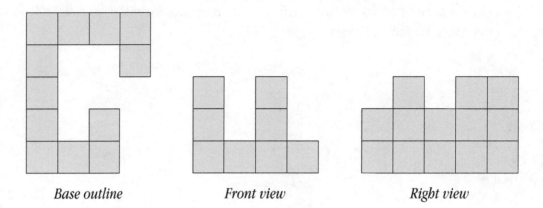

Base outline   *Front view*   *Right view*

Mathematical Reflections

In this investigation, you have built models to consider what additional constraint, or requirement, can be added to a set of building plans so it will specify only one building. These questions will help you summarize what you have learned:

1 Is it possible to build several buildings that fit a set of plans made up of a base outline, a front view, and a right view? Explain and illustrate your answer.

2 Is it possible for there to be a set of plans with the three views—base outline, front view, and right view—that has only one possible building? If so, how is this building different from the example you gave in question 1?

3 What can you require that will make every set of plans specify only one building? Explain why this requirement will give a unique building.

Think about your answers to these questions, discuss your ideas with other students and your teacher, and then write a summary of your findings in your journal.

Isometric Dot Paper Representations

In the last investigation, you learned how a set of building plans represents a unique maximal building. You also found that a set of building plans may correspond to several different minimal buildings.

In this investigation, you will learn about another way to represent three-dimensional cube buildings on paper. You will learn how to look at a cube building from a corner and make a drawing that shows three of its faces.

The Flat Iron building in New York City has an interesting corner.

You have used grid paper and dot paper in your mathematics classes to help you make graphs, record rectangles, and find areas. In this investigation, you will use a new kind of dot paper that will help you make drawings of the way buildings look from their corners. This new paper is called *isometric dot paper.* The word *isometric* comes from the Greek language and has two parts: "iso" meaning "the same," and "metric" meaning "measure." So isometric means "same measure."

4.1 ## Drawing a Cube

Below is part of a sheet of isometric dot paper. Take a few minutes to study the paper. Why do you think it is called isometric dot paper?

Think about this!

- Describe the pattern of dots on isometric dot paper. How is it different from the pattern on the usual kind of dot paper?

- Focus on a dot and the six dots that are its "nearest neighbors." You may want to mark your center and the six surrounding dots so that you can find them easily. Find the number of degrees in each of the angles that you can form with any three of the dots that you marked (one of the dots must serve as the vertex of the angle).

- What are the side lengths of the smallest equilateral triangle you can make by connecting three dots?

- What other patterns do you see in the way the dots are arranged or in the measures of angles on isometric dot paper?

Problem 4.1

Hold a cube level with your eyes. Look at the cube carefully. Turn it to see each of its corners. Tip the cube so that you see the corner nearest you in the center with six vertices evenly spaced around this center corner. Your challenge is to find a way to draw the cube in exactly this position on a sheet of isometric dot paper.

When you and your partner have each successfully drawn the cube, try to find a way to show a different view of the cube in a picture on the dot paper. The two pictures should look quite different. One should show the top of the cube and one should show the bottom.

■ Problem 4.1 Follow-Up

What is the measure of each angle of the cube drawn on dot paper? How do these measures compare to the measures on the real cube?

4.2 Drawing a Cube Model

Some people find it very hard to visualize cube models as they are pictured on isometric dot paper. To help you investigate drawing cube models on isometric dot paper, cut out the 2-D models of cubes on Labsheet 4.2. Store the models in an envelope so you don't lose them.

These models are like the drawing you made on isometric dot paper. If you turn a 2-D model upside down, you should see the drawing you made of the bottom of a cube. You can use the models to help you in Problem 4.2. Notice how the 2-D model can be placed to fit the dots on the isometric dot paper.

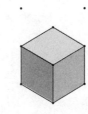

Problem 4.2

Make a stack using three cubes. Hold the stack in the air and turn it, observing it from many different views.

  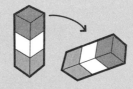

Your challenge is to find every way this stack of three cubes can be pictured on isometric dot paper.

You can use your 2-D cube models to help you draw your pictures. Be sure you stack the models in the same way that the real cubes are stacked. You can place the 2-D models on the dot paper so you can better see where to draw the lines.

Talk to your partner and check each other's work so that you can both get better at drawing models of cube arrangements on isometric dot paper.

■ **Problem 4.2 Follow-Up**

Describe any patterns you see in the isometric drawings of the stack of three cubes.

Drawing More Complex Buildings

Now that you have an idea of how to draw stacks of cubes and how to use your 2-D cube models to help you make drawings, you can try your skills on more complicated arrangements of cubes. In this problem, you will make drawings of cube buildings made from four cubes.

Problem 4.3

A. Use four cubes to make the building shown below. On isometric dot paper, make as many drawings of this cube building, turned in the air in different ways, as you can.

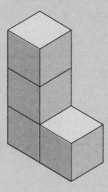

B. Explain why you think you have found all possible ways to draw the building on isometric dot paper.

■ Problem 4.3 Follow-Up

Now, make a different arrangement with four cubes. On dot paper, draw as many pictures as you can of your cube arrangement turned in different ways. Remember that the 2-D cube models can help you figure out what lines to connect on the dot paper.

4.4 Creating Your Own Building

Now it is your turn to be the architect. As you make drawings of your own building, think about what information someone else will be able to tell about your building from your drawings.

Problem 4.4

A. On your building mat, create a building using at least 7 cubes but no more than 12 cubes. Make a drawing of it on isometric dot paper. Label the drawing to indicate which corner the building is being viewed from (front right, right back, back left, or left front).

B. Now turn the building and make a drawing from the opposite corner. Label the view to indicate the corner.

C. If you give a friend just these two drawings, do you think he or she will be able to construct the building exactly as you have made it? Explain.

D. Exchange the isometric dot paper drawings that you made with the drawings that your partner made. Construct a cube building from your partner's drawings.

E. Were you able to get enough information from the drawings to re-create the building your partner constructed? Explain why or why not.

F. Was your partner able to re-create your building from your drawings? Why or why not?

G. In the last investigation, you found that a set of building plans does not always allow you to construct a unique building. However, if you specify that the building must be maximal, it will be unique. Do you think a set of two diagrams on isometric dot paper corresponds to a unique building? Or, is it possible that more than one building can be made from a set of two diagrams on isometric dot paper?

■ Problem 4.4 Follow-Up

Would a set of diagrams showing all four corners of a building determine a unique building? Explain your reasoning.

As you work on these ACE questions, use your calculator whenever you need it.

Applications

In 1–4, a view is shown from the front right corner of a building.

- Copy each building, exactly as it appears, on isometric dot paper.

- Make a cube model of the building. Then, make a drawing from the back left corner of the building.

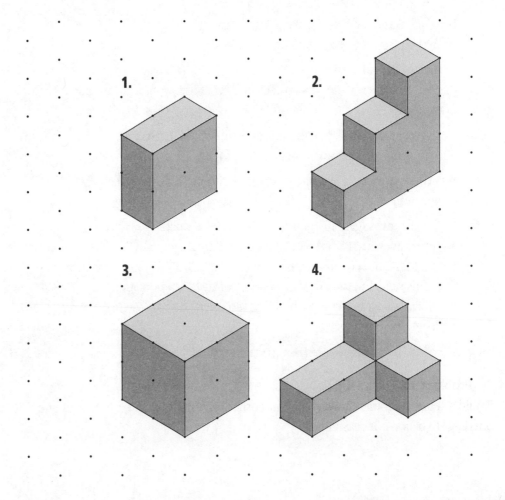

1.

2.

3.

4.

Connections

5. a. Use cubes to construct a model of each building in questions 1–4. For each building, draw a set of building plans on a sheet of grid paper.

b. Is there more than one building that will fit the building plans you have made? Why or why not?

Extensions

6. How many cubes touch the orange cube face to facc?

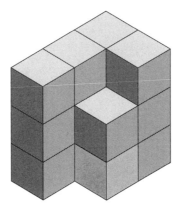

7. How many cubes are needed to build this rectangular solid?

Mathematical Reflections

In this investigation, you used isometric dot paper to learn a new way to make representations, or drawings, of cube buildings. These questions will help you summarize what you have learned:

1 Explain, in your own words, how isometric dot paper is arranged so that it is possible to draw cube buildings from the corners.

2 **a.** What are the measures of the angles formed by the edges of a face of a *real* cube?

b. On isometric dot paper, what are the measures of the angles formed by the edges of a cube?

c. Explain any differences or similarities in the measures you found.

3 Imagine that your friend gives you isometric drawings from all four corners of a cube building. Will you be able to read enough information to construct a building exactly like the original? Why or why not?

Think about your answers to these questions, discuss your ideas with other students and your teacher, and then write a summary of your findings in your journal.

Ziggurats

In this unit, you have learned three different ways to represent cube buildings with drawings. You can draw a *base plan* to record a building you have made; then, a friend can use your base plan to construct a replica of your building. You have also learned to make *a set of building plans,* which includes the base outline, the front view, and the right view of a building. Finally, you have learned to represent a building with an *isometric dot paper drawing,* which shows three sides of the building at once. In this investigation, you will use what you have learned to explore a special kind of pyramid that Emily Hawkins discovered among the ancient ruins of Montarek.

5.1 Building Ziggurats

Emily Hawkins found several pyramids among the ruins. She made a sketch of one of the pyramids using isometric dot paper.

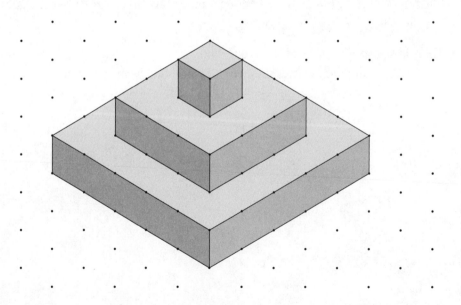

Notice that the pyramid has a square layer for each of its stories and that each layer is smaller than the layer beneath it. This kind of pyramid is called a *ziggurat* (pronounced *zig´-gu-rat*). Look up the word in your dictionary.

Did you know?

Archaelogists have uncovered over 30 ziggurats, some dating back to 3000 B.C., at sites in every important ancient Mesopotamian city. Ziggurats were built through great communal efforts as artificial mountains to house their local gods. Most of the ziggurats contained from three to seven levels. Sometimes the walls were painted different colors and plants and trees were grown on the terraces. This five-layer ziggurat built in the 13th century B.C. in the city of Tchoga Zanbil had a base of 122,500 square feet and was 174 feet high.

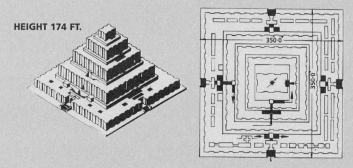

HEIGHT 174 FT.

Used with permission from the British Architectural Library, RIBA, London.

Problem 5.1

A. Make the base plan for the ziggurat shown on page 62.

B. Working with a partner, build the ziggurat with cubes, and make a set of building plans for it.

C. Why do you suppose people from ancient Montarek would build such pyramids? Explain your thoughts.

■ Problem 5.1 Follow-Up

1. List the numbers of cubes in each layer of the ziggurat from the top layer to the bottom layer. Is there a pattern in this sequence? Explain your answer.

2. If the ziggurat in Problem 5.1 had a fourth and fifth layer of cubes added to the bottom, how many cubes would be needed for each of these new layers? Explain your reasoning.

5.2 Representing Ziggurats

Emily Hawkins found that the ziggurat pyramids of Montarek were not all the same size. Some were small; others were quite huge. She has uncovered different base plans of two ziggurats.

Problem 5.2

Below are sketches of base plans that Emily Hawkins found in the diary of an architect who was a citizen of ancient Montarek.

1	1	1
1	2	1
1	1	1

Front

3	3	3	3	3
3	5	5	5	3
3	5	6	5	3
3	5	5	5	3
3	3	3	3	3

Front

A. Construct a model of the first ziggurat from cubes. Then, use your model to sketch a set of building plans for the ziggurat on grid paper.

B. Use cubes to construct a model of the second ziggurat. Make a sketch of the ziggurat on isometric dot paper. Look back at the ziggurat from Problem 5.1 if you are unsure of how to begin.

C. Compare the representations you have made of the two ziggurats. Write a short paragraph explaining to Emily which of the three representations—the cube model, the building plans, or the sketch on isometric dot paper—is the most useful for describing a ziggurat.

■ Problem 5.2 Follow-Up

Design a ziggurat in which each layer is more than one cube thick. Draw a base plan for your ziggurat.

As you work on these ACE questions, use your calculator whenever you need it.

Applications

1. Some of the buildings in Montarek are shaped something like a ziggurat, but not exactly. Here is a sketch from the front right corner of an ancient Montarek building:

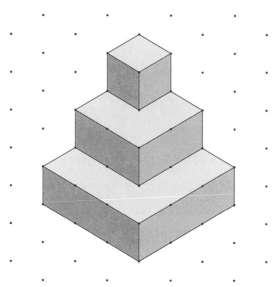

   a. Make a cube model of the building and draw a base plan of your model on grid paper.

   b. Make a set of building plans for the building on grid paper.

   c. Make an isometric drawing of the building from the corner opposite the one above.

   d. How would you describe the building? Write a brief paragraph that explains how the building is different from a ziggurat and how it is similar to a ziggurat. Also describe what you think the building might have been used for.

2. Which of the following is *not* a corner view of the building represented by the base plan?

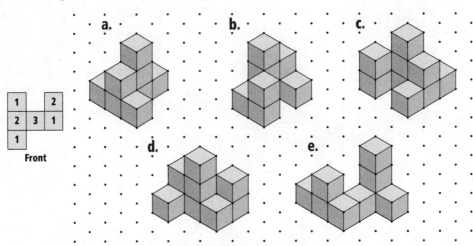

1		2
2	3	1
1		

Front

a.

b.

c.

d.

e.

3. Which drawing below shows the building represented in the base plan viewed from the *front left* corner?

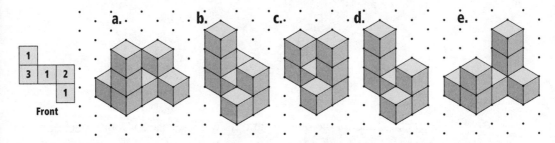

1		
3	1	2
	1	

Front

a.

b.

c.

d.

e.

4. The drawing on the left shows one view of a building. Find another view of the building.

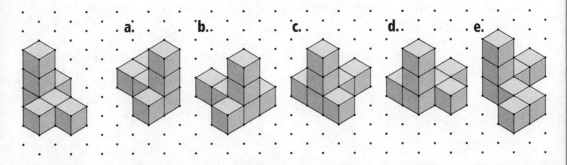

a.

b.

c.

d.

e.

Connections

5. Choose a building in your community. Make a sketch of the building on isometric dot paper. When you are finished with your sketch, answer the following questions:

a. Is it possible to copy the building exactly on isometric dot paper? Explain how you made your sketch, including any assumptions or simplifications you made.

b. You will have to guess, but try to build a cube model that looks like a good representation of the building. (If it has a slanted roof, make a model without the roof.) Make a set of building plans for the building.

Houston, Texas

Extensions

6. Emily Hawkins discovered the remains of an interesting building among the ruins of ancient Montarek. Below is a base plan of the building:

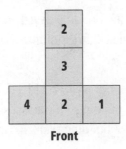

Front

a. Make a cube model of the building. Then, on isometric dot paper, make sketches of the building as it is viewed from each corner—the front right corner, the right back corner, the back left corner, and the left front corner. Label each sketch.

b. On grid paper, make a base plan that is different from the one above, but that represents a building that looks the same as the original when sketched from the front right corner. Explain why the building made from your new base plan would look the same as the original building on dot paper.

The ruins of the Incan city of Machu-Picchu in Peru

7. Using five cubes, make a figure in the shape of a cross. Imagine that the figure can turn in any direction in space, including upside down. Find *every* different way this figure can be drawn on isometric dot paper. Explain why you think you have found all the possible views. Two are shown here as examples:

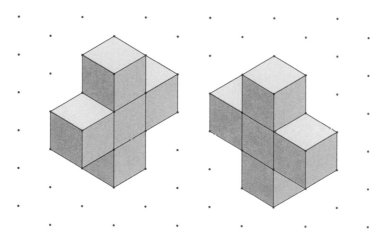

8. Make a T-shaped figure from five cubes. Imagine that the figure can turn in any direction in space. Find *every* different way this figure can be drawn on isometric dot paper. Explain why you think you have found all the possible views.

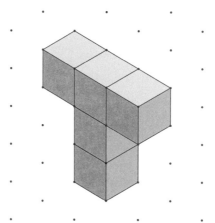

9. Look carefully at each of the following building diagrams:

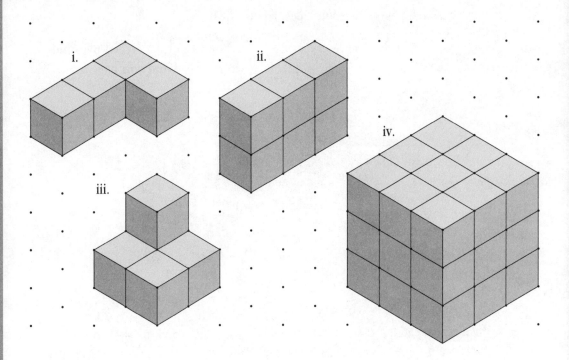

The *volume* of a cube building is a measure of how many *cubic units* it takes to *fill* the building. In other words, the number of cubes needed to make a cube model of a building is the volume of the building.

a. Without making cube models, find the volume of each building above—record how many cubes it would take to construct each of the buildings. If there are different numbers of cubes that could be used to construct a building, list all the possibilities, and explain why the different volumes are possible.

b. Without making cube models, record the perimeter of the base of each of the buildings. As in part a, if there is more than one perimeter possible for a building, list all the possibilities.

Mathematical Reflections

In this investigation you have sketched and examined special kinds of pyramids called ziggurats. These questions will help you summarize what you have learned:

1. Describe a ziggurat.

2. If a cube model of a ziggurat has five layers, each one cube thick, and the top layer is a single cube, how many cubes will it take to make the model? Explain why you think you are correct.

Think about your answers to these questions, discuss your ideas with other students and your teacher, and then write a summary of your findings in your journal. Be sure to include sketches if you think they would help your comments make more sense.

Seeing the Isometric View

This investigation will help you improve your ability to read isometric drawings. During this investigation, you will have the opportunity to think about the following:

• How can a drawing help you to visualize the building it describes?
• Can you use your imagination to visualize what a building will look like after some small alteration is made to it?

6.1 Viewing a Building

You have learned to draw isometric representations showing each of the four corners of a building. But can you interpret a drawing that someone else has done? Can you compare the drawing to cube models and identify which model it describes? Can you determine which corner of the building is shown in the picture?

Problem 6.1

In your group, build a cube model of each of these buildings on your building mat. The next page shows views of each building from all four corners. These views also appear on Labsheet 6.1. Match each model to its corner views. On the labsheet, label each view with the building number and the corner from which the building is being viewed: left front, front right, back left, or right back.

Building 1

1	1	2
	3	1
	1	

Front

Building 2

1	1	2
1	3	
	1	

Front

Building 3

1	2	1
	3	1
	2	

Front

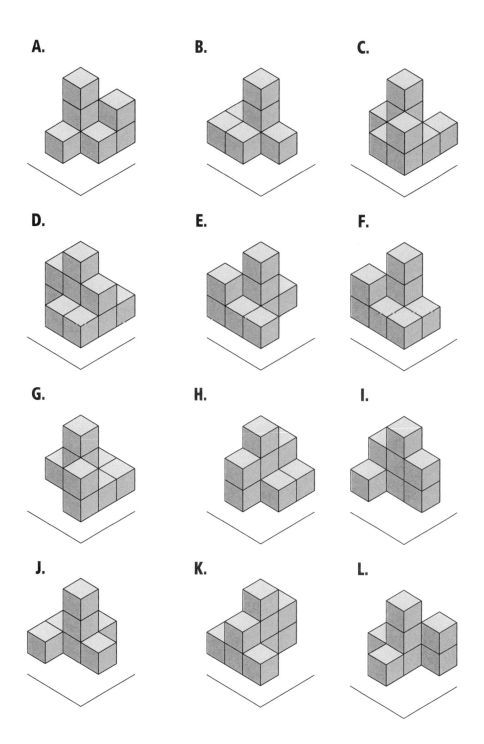

A.

B.

C.

D.

E.

F.

G.

H.

I.

J.

K.

L.

■ **Problem 6.1 Follow-Up**

Can you remove a cube from building 1 and have the isometric view from any corner still be the same? What about building 2 and building 3?

6.2 Removing Cubes

In this problem, you will play with a building in your mind to visualize what it would look like if you removed cubes from it. As you work on this problem, remember that you can always build a cube model to check your imagination—but give your mind a try first. You will be surprised at how much you can improve your visualization skills by thinking hard about the problems and by practicing visualizing things in your mind.

Problem 6.2

In each drawing given, visualize what the figure would look like if the orange cubes were removed. Make an isometric drawing of the result. If you need to, build the model from cubes and look at it.

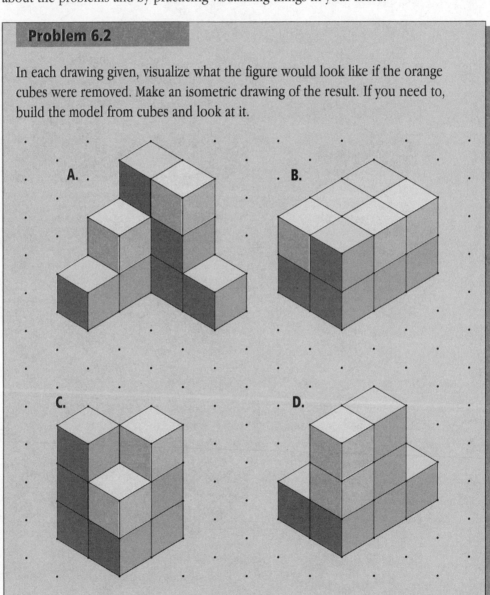

■ Problem 6.2 Follow-Up

Look carefully at A–D. Can you find a different possibility for what the building would look like with orange cubes removed?

6.3 Adding Cubes

In the last problem, you imagined what cube buildings would look like if some cubes were removed. In this problem, you will imagine what buildings will look like if cubes are added. Remember to try to do the problem without cubes first. Then, you can build a model to check your work.

Problem 6.3

In each drawing, one or more cube faces are orange. Picture what the model would look like with a cube added to each orange face. Make an isometric drawing of the result.

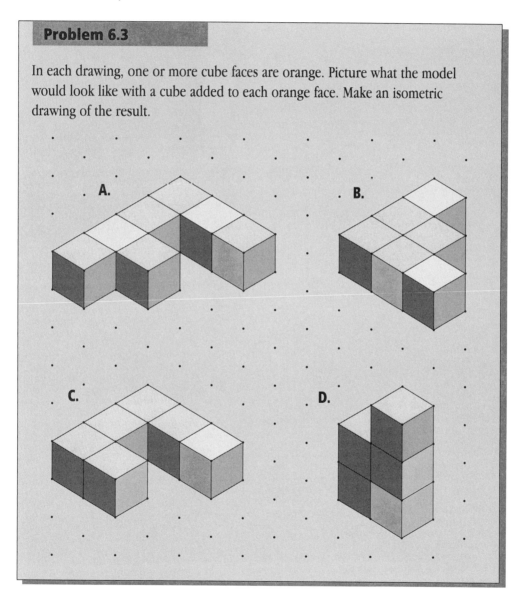

■ Problem 6.3 Follow-Up

Which is harder for you to visualize and draw without building a cube model, adding or removing a cube? Explain why you think this is so.

Putting the Pieces Together

In this problem, you will look at several buildings made from these two basic shapes:

Your challenge is to figure out how these two shapes were put together to make each building.

   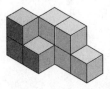

Problem 6.4

In A–F, experiment with the two basic shapes above to make the building shown. Shade the drawings on your labsheet to show how you put the pieces together to make the shape.

A.

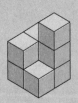

B.

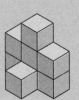

C.

D.

E.

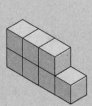

F.

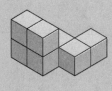

■ Problem 6.4 Follow-Up

Put the two basic shapes together in a way not shown above. Make an isometric drawing of your model.

Applications

1. On a building mat, use cubes to make a model of this building.

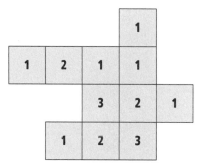

Front

a. For each picture below, indicate from which corner you are viewing the building.

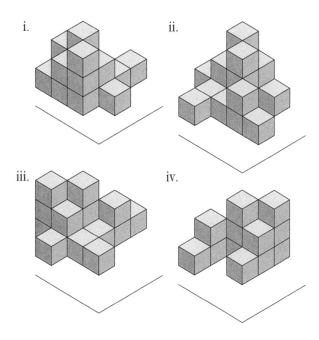

i.

ii.

iii.

iv.

b. Remove a cube from each of the three stacks in the front row of the base plan. Make isometric drawings of all four corners of this new building.

c. Do any of the corner views stay the same as the corresponding corner view on the original building?

2. Visualize what this model would look like with the orange cubes removed. Draw an isometric view of the resulting model from the same corner as the original drawing was made.

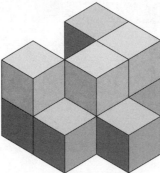

3. Visualize what this model would look like if cubes were added to the orange faces. Draw an isometric view of the resulting model from the same corner as the original model was made.

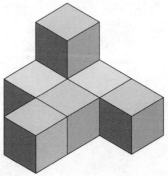

4. Design your own two basic shapes. Use four or five cubes for each shape. Put the shapes together to make a new model. Draw the shapes and the new model on isometric dot paper so that you can challenge a classmate to find how you put the two pieces together.

Connections

5. Talk to your art teacher, a drafting teacher, or an architect about the kind of drawings they make. Report on the similarities and differences between their drawings and the kinds of drawings you have made in this unit.

Extensions

6. Here is a drawing of a simple model made from cubes:

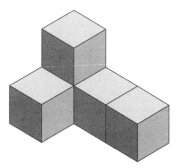

    a. How many cubes are in the model?

    b. What is the perimeter of the base of the model?

Imagine a model just like the one above but with each of its edge lengths doubled.

    c. How many cubes would it take to build the new model?

    d. What is the perimeter of the base of the new model?

    e. Make an isometric drawing of the new model from the same corner the drawing of the original model was made from.

7. a. The building below is shown from the front right corner. How many cubes would it take to make this building? If there is more than one answer, give the least and the greatest numbers of cubes that could be used.

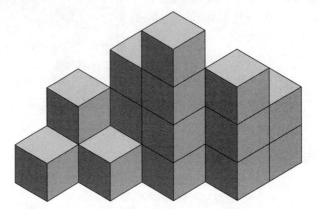

b. Make a base plan for a building made with the minimum number of cubes.

c. Make a base plan for the building made with the maximum number of cubes.

Mathematical Reflections

In this investigation, you have worked on visualizing corner views of buildings, even when the buildings are changed by adding or removing cubes. These questions will help you summarize what you have learned:

1 Summarize how you look at a model built from cubes to see the model in a way that can be drawn on isometric dot paper.

2 If you make an isometric drawing of a model from each of its four corners, will your drawings determine a unique building? Explain why or why not. You may want to use an example in your explanation.

Think about your answers to these questions, discuss your ideas with other students and your teacher, and then write a summary of your findings in your journal.

Design a Building

According to the diary of an architect in ancient Montarek, a building had to be approved by the Council of Montarek before it could be constructed. To have a building approved, an architect had to provide the council with a base plan, a set of building plans, and isometric sketches of the building.

Imagine that you are an architect in ancient Montarek. Design a building that you feel would be useful to the citizens of Montarek. The building does not have to be a ziggurat or any of the other buildings you have studied. This is your opportunity to design a building that *you* think is interesting.

You must follow these steps to have your building approved by the Council of Montarek:

1. Use 25 to 30 cubes to design your building.
2. Make a base plan of your building on grid paper.
3. Make a set of building plans for your building on grid paper.
4. Make four sketches of your building on isometric dot paper—one sketch from each corner.
5. Write a paragraph to the Council of Montarek explaining how your building could be used and why it would benefit the citizens of Montarek.

Looking Back and Looking Ahead

Unit Reflections

Working on problems in this unit helped you to develop your spatial visualization skills. You learned how to read and draw two-dimensional *isometric drawings,* *outline views,* and *base-plans* for three-dimensional buildings and how to build three-dimensional buildings from two-dimensional representations.

Using Your Visualization Skills—Test your spatial reasoning and drawing skills on the following problems.

1. *The following figure is an isometric drawing showing the front-right view of a building made from cubes. Assume that you can see parts of every cube used to build the figure.*

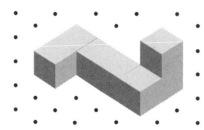

   a. Make a base plan for the building.

   b. If you were to glue the cubes together, how many cube faces would there be on the outside of the resulting building?

2. *A building made from cubes has the base, front, and right views shown below.*

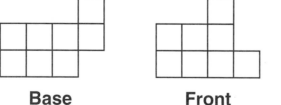

| Base | Front | Right |

a. How many cubes are needed to construct a minimal building for these plans?

b. How many cubes are needed to construct a maximal building for these plans?

c. Draw base plans for your answers to part a and part b.

3 *The base plan for a building made from cubes is given at the right. On isometric dot paper, draw the view of that building from the left-front corner.*

Back

	1	
2	1	
3	2	1

Left   Right

Front

Explaining Your Reasoning—To answer questions about figures made from cubes, you need spatial visualization skills and reasoning.

1. How do you look at a building in order to draw it on isometric dot paper?

2. How do you prepare base, front, and right outline views of a building?

3. How do you analyze a building to make a base plan?

4. How do you build a model from cubes if you are given

    a. an isometric view?

    b. outline views from the base, front, and right of the building?

5. Is there more than one way to make a building of cubes from a given

    a. base plan?

    b. isometric drawing?

    c. set of base, front, and right outline views?

The spatial visualization skills you developed in this unit will be useful in future *Connected Mathematics* units, especially in work on problems about surface area, volume, and symmetry of solid figures. Two-dimensional drawings, photographs, and computer displays are the standard ways of picturing three-dimensional scenes. So, ability to add depth mentally to those images is also useful in many practical and technical tasks.

Glossary

base plan A drawing of the base outline of a building. The number in each square indicates the number of cubes in the stack at that position.

building mat A sheet of paper labeled "front", "back", "left", and "right" used to describe buildings.

isometric dot paper Dot paper in which the distance from a dot to each of the six surrounding dots are all equivalent. The word *isometric* comes from the Greek words *iso*, which means "same," and *metric*, which means "measure." You used isometric dot paper to show different views of your cube models.

line of symmetry A line through a figure so that if the figure were folded on the line, the two parts of the figure would match up exactly.

maximal building The building satisfying a given set of building plans and having the largest possible number of cubes. There is only one possible maximal building for a set of plans, and so this building is called unique.

minimal building A building satisfying a given set of plans and having the smallest possible number of cubes. Because there may be several minimal buildings for a set of plans, the minimal building is not necessarily unique.

set of building plans A set of three diagrams—the front view, the right view, and the base outline.

unique One of a kind. When we say that the building corresponding to a set of plans is unique, we mean that it is the only building that matches the plans.

ziggurat A pyramid-shaped building made up of layers in which each layer is a square smaller than the square beneath it.

Glosario

alfombrilla para construcción Una hoja de papel rotulada "frente", "atrás", "izquierda" y "derecha" usada para describir edificios.

conjunto de planos de construcción Un conjunto de tres diagramas: la vista de frente, la vista de la derecha y el contorno de la base.

edificio máximo El edificio que satisface un conjunto dado de planos de construcción y que tiene el mayor número posible de cubos. Hay sólo un edificio máximo posible para un conjunto de planos, por eso este edificio se llama único.

edificio mínimo Un edificio que satisface un conjunto dado de planos y que tiene el menor número posible de cubos. Como puede haber varios edificios mínimos para un conjunto de planos, el edificio mínimo no es necesariamente único.

eje de simetría Una línea a través una figura de manera que si la figura se doblara sobre el eje o línea, las dos partes de la figura coincidirían exactamente.

plano de la base Un dibujo del contorno de la base de un edificio. El número que aparece en cada cuadrado indica el número de cubos que hay en la pila en esa posición.

trama punteada isométrica Papel punteado en el cual las distancias desde un punto hasta cada uno de los seis puntos que lo rodean son todas equivalentes. La palabra "isométrica" viene de las palabras griegas *iso*, que significa "igual", y *métrica*, que significa "medida". Has usado papel de trama punteada isométrica para mostrar diferentes vistas de tus modelos de cubos.

único Uno de una clase. Cuando decimos que el edificio que corresponde a un conjunto de planos es único, queremos decir que es el único edificio que coincide con los planos.

zigurat Un edificio con forma de pirámide hecha en capas, en el que cada capa es un cuadrado más pequeño que el cuadrado que está debajo.

Index